D0560619

MY FINAL ANSWER FOR KIDS

TWENTY QUIZZES THAT PUT *KIDS* IN THE HOT SEAT

PAUL KENT

BARBOUR BOOKS
An Imprint of Barbour Publishing, Inc.

MY FINAL ANSWER FOR KIDS

© 2002 by Barbour Publishing, Inc.

ISBN 1-58660-500-3

All rights reserved. No part of this publication may be reproduced or transmitted in any form or by any means without written permission of the publisher.

All Scripture quotations are taken from the HOLY BIBLE: NEW INTERNATIONAL VERSION ®. NIV ®. Copyright © 1973, 1978, 1984 by International Bible Society. Used by permission of Zondervan Publishing House. All rights reserved.

Published by Barbour Books, an imprint of Barbour Publishing, Inc., P.O. Box 719, Uhrichsville, Ohio 44683
www.barbourbooks.com

Printed in the United States of America.
5 4 3 2

ACKNOWLEDGMENTS

Special thanks to
the Junior Church crew
at Dover Bible:

Amber, Brittany, Caitlin,
Heather, Jennie, Jennifer,
Josh, Nate, Rae Ann, Samantha R.,
Samantha W., and Taylor

INTRODUCTION

Hey, kids—here's the Bible trivia book you've been waiting for: *My Final Answer for Kids*! How much do you *really* know about the Bible? Find out in these twenty brand-new quizzes!

Each quiz has six levels of multiple-choice questions, beginning with some really easy stuff. But the questions get harder as you move up through the levels. If you can get through the first two questions without a miss, you'll win Bible Bronze. If you can answer four questions correctly, you'll earn Bible Silver. And if you have the smarts to complete all six questions without a wrong answer, you'll win Bible Gold! But watch out—you'll have to know your Bible stories awfully well to answer the higher-level questions!

You will have help, though. Once in each quiz, you can:

Double Your Chances: Look up this bonus to learn two of the wrong answers. . .

or

Look in the Book: Look up this bonus for the question's Bible reference. . . then find your final answer in the Good Book itself!

Remember—you get a total of two Bible Bonuses (one of each) in each six-question quiz. The answer to each question is on the following page, along with some fun "Did You Know?" questions.

So are you ready for the challenge? Step up to the "hot seat" and show us your Bible knowledge! It's interesting, it's fun, it's *My Final Answer for Kids*!

TWENTY QUIZZES THAT PUT KIDS IN THE HOT SEAT.
BIBLE
TRIVIA

QUIZ 1

LEVEL 1

Where did the prophet Jonah spend three strange days and nights?

a) on a spaceship
b) in an eagle's nest
c) under a waterfall
d) inside a fish

BIBLE BONUSES

Double Your Chances: A and C

Look in the Book: Jonah 1:17

LEVEL 1

Where did the prophet Jonah spend three strange days and nights?

a) on a spaceship
b) in an eagle's nest
c) under a waterfall
d) inside a fish

DID YOU KNOW?

Jesus once said that He would be like Jonah: "As Jonah was three days and three nights in the belly of a huge fish, so the Son of Man will be three days and three nights in the heart of the earth" (Matthew 12:40). Jesus was talking about the time He would be killed and put in a tomb, but three days later come back to life.

QUIZ 1

BIBLE BRONZE

What were Peter and Andrew doing when Jesus asked them to be His disciples?

a) playing chess
b) building a house
c) fishing
d) cooking dinner

BIBLE BONUSES

Double Your Chances: A and D

Look in the Book: Matthew 4:1–19

BIBLE BRONZE

What were Peter and Andrew doing when Jesus asked them to be His disciples?

a) playing chess
b) building a house
c) fishing
d) cooking dinner

DID YOU KNOW?

Jesus said the famous words "I will make you fishers of men" to Peter and Andrew.

LEVEL 3

What famous man was the brother of the Old Testament priest Aaron?

a) Moses
b) Abraham
c) Joseph
d) Adam

BIBLE BONUSES

Double Your Chances: B and C

Look in the Book: Exodus 4:14

LEVEL 3

What famous man was the brother of the Old Testament priest Aaron?

a) **Moses**
b) Abraham
c) Joseph
d) Adam

DID YOU KNOW?

Moses didn't like his own voice—so God said that Aaron would speak for Moses. Look it up in Exodus 6:28–7:2.

BIBLE SILVER

What color horse does Jesus ride during the great battle in the book of Revelation?

a) gold
b) red
c) white
d) black

BIBLE BONUSES

Double Your Chances: B and D

Look in the Book: Revelation 19:11

BIBLE SILVER

What color horse does Jesus ride during the great battle in the book of Revelation?

a) gold
b) red
c) white
d) black

DID YOU KNOW?

The color white stands for things that are pure—like God and Jesus. Daniel says God's clothing is "white as snow," and His hair "white like wool" (Daniel 7:9). In Revelation 20:11, God sits on a "great white throne."

LEVEL 5

Who is Michael in the New Testament?

a) a disciple of Jesus
b) a Roman governor
c) an archangel
d) the author of Galatians

BIBLE BONUSES

Double Your Chances: A and D

Look in the Book: Jude 9

LEVEL 5

Who is Michael in the New Testament?

a) a disciple of Jesus
b) a Roman governor
c) an archangel
d) the author of Galatians

DID YOU KNOW?

The word *arch* can mean "the most important"—so an *archangel* is "the most important angel."

BIBLE GOLD

Who was stoned to death as the first person to be killed for following Jesus?

a) John
b) James
c) Philip
d) Stephen

BIBLE BONUSES

Double Your Chances: B and C

Look in the Book: Acts 7:59–60

BIBLE GOLD

Who was stoned to death as the first person to be killed for following Jesus?

a) John
b) James
c) Philip
d) Stephen

DID YOU KNOW?

A person who is killed for following Jesus is called a *martyr*.

QUIZ 2

LEVEL 1

How did God destroy the wicked people of the earth during Noah's time?

a) with a giant tornado
b) with a giant fire
c) with a giant flood
d) with a giant

BIBLE BONUSES

Double Your Chances: B and D

Look in the Book: Genesis 7:17–22

LEVEL 1

How did God destroy the wicked people of the earth during Noah's time?

a) with a giant tornado
b) with a giant fire
c) with a giant flood
d) with a giant

DID YOU KNOW?

Jesus said that His second coming will be like Noah's flood. "In the days before the flood," Jesus said, "people were eating and drinking, marrying and giving in marriage, up to the day Noah entered the ark; and they knew nothing about what would happen until the flood came and took them all away. That is how it will be at the coming of the Son of Man" (Matthew 24:38–39).

QUIZ 2

BIBLE BRONZE

What kind of tree did Zacchaeus climb in order to see Jesus?

a) palm
b) oak
c) sycamore
d) crab apple

BIBLE BONUSES

Double Your Chances: A and D

Look in the Book: Luke 19:4

BIBLE BRONZE

What kind of tree did Zacchaeus climb in order to see Jesus?

a) palm
b) oak
c) sycamore
d) crab apple

DID YOU KNOW?

God gave His people, the Israelites, some special rules about trees. When the people of Israel were fighting against a city, God told them, "Do not destroy its trees by putting an ax to them, because you can eat their fruit. Do not cut them down. Are the trees of the field people, that you should besiege them?" (Deuteronomy 20:19).

LEVEL 3

What is Methuselah famous for?

a) He was Adam and Eve's favorite movie star.
b) He was thrown into the fiery furnace.
c) He was brought back to life by Elijah.
d) He lived 969 years.

BIBLE BONUSES

Double Your Chances: A and B

Look in the Book: Genesis 5:27

LEVEL 3

What is Methuselah famous for?

a) He was Adam and Eve's favorite movie star.
b) He was thrown into the fiery furnace.
c) He was brought back to life by Elijah.
d) He lived 969 years.

DID YOU KNOW?

The Guinness Book of World Records says the oldest person in recent times was Jeanne Calment of France. When she died in 1997, she was 122 years old!

BIBLE SILVER

What did Jesus say His love for Christians would be like?

a) a man with his son
b) a shepherd with his sheep
c) a king with his queen
d) a bear with her cub

BIBLE BONUSES

Double Your Chances: C and D

Look in the Book: John 10:14

BIBLE SILVER

What did Jesus say His love for Christians would be like?

a) a man with his son
b) **a shepherd with his sheep**
c) a king with his queen
d) a bear with her cub

DID YOU KNOW?

Jesus said a good shepherd knows all of his sheep by name, and the sheep know their shepherd's voice (John 10:3–4)—and that's just like Jesus with His followers!

LEVEL 5

Which disciple said he needed proof to believe that Jesus had come back to life?

a) Thomas
b) John
c) Simon the Zealot
d) Peter

BIBLE BONUSES

Double Your Chances: B and C

Look in the Book: John 20:24–25

LEVEL 5

Which disciple said he needed proof to believe that Jesus had come back to life?

a) **Thomas**
b) John
c) Simon the Zealot
d) Peter

DID YOU KNOW?

The nickname "Doubting Thomas" comes from this disciple!

BIBLE GOLD

How many years did Jacob agree to work to have Rachel as his wife?

a) 1
b) 7
c) 20
d) 100

BIBLE BONUSES

Double Your Chances: C and D

Look in the Book: Genesis 29:18

BIBLE GOLD

How many years did Jacob agree to work to have Rachel as his wife?

a) 1
b) 7
c) 20
d) 100

DID YOU KNOW?

Jacob agreed to work seven years for Rachel, but ended up working *fourteen* years for her—because Rachel's father tricked Jacob into marrying Rachel's older sister first. Check out the whole story in Genesis 29:10–30.

QUIZ 3

LEVEL 1

What huge man lost a fight with a boy named David?

a) Ishbi-Benob
b) Goliath
c) Saph
d) The Jolly Green Giant

BIBLE BONUSES

Double Your Chances: A and D

Look in the Book: 1 Samuel 17:4, 50

LEVEL 1

What huge man lost a fight with a boy named David?

a) Ishbi-Benob
b) **Goliath**
c) Saph
d) The Jolly Green Giant

DID YOU KNOW?

Goliath wasn't the only giant bad guy of the Bible. . .check out 2 Samuel 21:15–22 for details on some others—including a guy with twenty-four fingers and toes!

BIBLE BRONZE

What king was known around the world for his wisdom?

a) Solomon
b) Nebuchadnezzar
c) Agrippa
d) Burger King

BIBLE BONUSES

Double Your Chances: C and D

Look in the Book: 1 Kings 4:24–29

BIBLE BRONZE

What king was known around the world for his wisdom?

a) **Solomon**
b) Nebuchadnezzar
c) Agrippa
d) Burger King

DID YOU KNOW?

Solomon was also a science teacher! In 1 Kings 4:33, the Bible says he "described plant life, from the cedar of Lebanon to the hyssop that grows out of walls. He also taught about animals and birds, reptiles and fish." Solomon was so interesting that people came from all over the world to listen to him.

LEVEL 3

What is the name for the stories Jesus told to teach people about God's kingdom?

a) miracles
b) parables
c) oracles
d) Lunchables

BIBLE BONUSES

Double Your Chances: A and D

Look in the Book: Matthew 13:34

LEVEL 3

What is the name for the stories Jesus told to teach people about God's kingdom?

a) miracles
b) parables
c) oracles
d) Lunchables

DID YOU KNOW?

Jesus' story about the Good Samaritan was a parable (Luke 10:30–37).

BIBLE SILVER

What problem was the brave army commander Naaman healed of?

a) blindness
b) leprosy
c) fever
d) a hunched back

BIBLE BONUSES

Double Your Chances: C and D

Look in the Book: 2 Kings 5:1, 14

BIBLE SILVER

What problem was the brave army commander Naaman healed of?

a) blindness
b) leprosy
c) fever
d) a hunched back

DID YOU KNOW?

Most people think of leprosy as a disease of the skin—but it can also affect the lungs and even cause blindness.

LEVEL 5

What did the people of Malta say about Paul when a snakebite didn't kill him?

a) that he was lucky
b) that he was a demon
c) that he was a god
d) that he was really tough

BIBLE BONUSES

Double Your Chances: B and D

Look in the Book: Acts 28:6

LEVEL 5

What did the people of Malta say about Paul when a snakebite didn't kill him?

a) that he was lucky
b) that he was a demon
c) that he was a god
d) that he was really tough

DID YOU KNOW?

Malta is an island in the Mediterranean Sea... and it has a place called "St. Paul's Bay."

BIBLE GOLD

Which of these women was a judge of Israel?

a) Deborah
b) Bathsheba
c) Esther
d) Rebekah

BIBLE BONUSES

Double Your Chances: B and C

Look in the Book: Judges 4:4

BIBLE GOLD

Which of these women was a judge of Israel?

a) **Deborah**
b) Bathsheba
c) Esther
d) Rebekah

DID YOU KNOW?

Deborah was also a leader in the army! She went into battle with a nervous commander named Barak, who told her, "If you go with me, I will go; but if you don't go with me, I won't go" (Judges 4:8).

QUIZ 4

LEVEL 1

What did Adam name his wife?

a) Madam
b) Abigail
c) Mary
d) Eve

BIBLE BONUSES

Double Your Chances: A and B

Look in the Book: Genesis 3:20

LEVEL 1

What did Adam name his wife?

a) Madam
b) Abigail
c) Mary
d) Eve

DID YOU KNOW?

Eve means "living."

BIBLE BRONZE

How many criminals were crucified with Jesus?

a) none
b) 1
c) 2
d) a dozen

BIBLE BONUSES

Double Your Chances: A and D

Look in the Book: Luke 23:32

BIBLE BRONZE

How many criminals were crucified with Jesus?

a) none
b) 1
c) 2
d) a dozen

DID YOU KNOW?

Jesus was crucified at the place called "Calvary." Be careful that you don't say "cavalry"—that's the part of an army that rides horses or trucks into battle!

LEVEL 3

What country suffered terrible plagues for keeping God's special people—the Israelites—as slaves?

a) Egypt
b) Babylon
c) Syria
d) Russia

BIBLE BONUSES

Double Your Chances: C and D

Look in the Book: Exodus 7:5

LEVEL 3

What country suffered terrible plagues for keeping God's special people—the Israelites—as slaves?

a) **Egypt**
b) Babylon
c) Syria
d) Russia

DID YOU KNOW?

Years before the plagues, Egypt had invited the Israelites to move in—because Egypt's ruler at that time, Joseph, was an Israelite. But later, a new king, "who did not know about Joseph" (Exodus 1:8), took over in Egypt and made life hard for the Israelites.

QUIZ 4

BIBLE SILVER

How did Jacob describe his brother Esau?

a) scary
b) wary
c) hairy
d) merry

BIBLE BONUSES

Double Your Chances: A and B

Look in the Book: Genesis 27:11

BIBLE SILVER

How did Jacob describe his brother Esau?

a) scary
b) wary
c) hairy
d) merry

DID YOU KNOW?

Esau was so hairy that his brother Jacob put on a goat skin to imitate him. Their blind father, Isaac, felt all of that goat fur and believed that Jacob, who had smooth skin, was really the hairy Esau! Read the whole story in Genesis 27:15–23.

LEVEL 5

What did Jesus drink while he was on the cross?

a) vinegar
b) milk
c) water
d) olive oil

BIBLE BONUSES

Double Your Chances: B and D

Look in the Book: John 19:29–30

LEVEL 5

What did Jesus drink while he was on the cross?

a) **vinegar**
b) milk
c) water
d) olive oil

DID YOU KNOW?

Grapes, rice, and other foods can be used to make vinegar.

QUIZ 4

BIBLE GOLD

What made King Saul stand out from rest of the Israelites?

a) He was stronger.
b) He had darker skin.
c) He was taller.
d) He had a nicer voice.

BIBLE BONUSES

Double Your Chances: B and D

Look in the Book: 1 Samuel 9:2

BIBLE GOLD

What made King Saul stand out from rest of the Israelites?

a) He was stronger.
b) He had darker skin.
c) He was taller.
d) He had a nicer voice.

DID YOU KNOW?

Saul was the very first king of Israel—about one thousand years before Jesus was born.

QUIZ 5

LEVEL 1

What miracle did Jesus do for His friend Lazarus?

a) brought him back to life
b) turned a stone into bread
c) healed him of leprosy
d) turned his spinach into ice cream

BIBLE BONUSES

Double Your Chances: C and D

Look in the Book: John 11:43–44

LEVEL 1

What miracle did Jesus do for His friend Lazarus?

a) **brought him back to life**
b) turned a stone into bread
c) healed him of leprosy
d) turned his spinach into ice cream

DID YOU KNOW?

The shortest verse in the Bible is found in the story of Lazarus. John 11:35 says that when He saw people crying over Lazarus, "Jesus wept."

QUIZ 5

BIBLE BRONZE

What did the people of Babel try to build to reach the heavens?

a) a rocket
b) a ladder
c) a staircase
d) a tower

BIBLE BONUSES

Double Your Chances: A and C

Look in the Book: Genesis 11:1–9

BIBLE BRONZE

What did the people of Babel try to build to reach the heavens?

a) a rocket
b) a ladder
c) a staircase
d) a tower

DID YOU KNOW?

The tallest building in the United States is the Sears Tower in Chicago, Illinois. It's more than a quarter of a mile high. . .but it doesn't reach to heaven!

LEVEL 3

What happened when Jesus sent demons out of a man and into a herd of pigs?

a) The pigs fought each other.
b) The pigs began to talk.
c) The pigs ran into a lake and drowned.
d) The pigs burst into flames.

BIBLE BONUSES

Double Your Chances: B and D

Look in the Book: Mark 5:11–13

LEVEL 3

What happened when Jesus sent demons out of a man and into a herd of pigs?

a) The pigs fought each other.
b) The pigs began to talk.
c) The pigs ran into a lake and drowned.
d) The pigs burst into flames.

DID YOU KNOW?

The people of Israel weren't allowed to eat ham, or bacon, or pork chops—anything that came from pigs. God had told them, in Leviticus 11:7–8, "The pig. . .is unclean for you. You must not eat their meat."

BIBLE SILVER

What did Jesus use to get Saul's attention on the road to Damascus?

a) a bright light
b) a whirlwind
c) an earthquake
d) a stampede of elephants

BIBLE BONUSES

Double Your Chances: B and D

Look in the Book: Acts 9:3–4

BIBLE SILVER

What did Jesus use to get Saul's attention on the road to Damascus?

a) **a bright light**
b) a whirlwind
c) an earthquake
d) a stampede of elephants

DID YOU KNOW?

Saul was on his way to *arrest* Christians, when God turned Saul himself into a Christian! Later, Saul was called "Paul" and wrote several of the books of the New Testament.

LEVEL 5

What strange vision did Ezekiel once have?

a) a tree in the middle of a tree
b) a box in the middle of a box
c) a wheel in the middle of a wheel
d) a star in the middle of a star

BIBLE BONUSES

Double Your Chances: A and B

Look in the Book: Ezekiel 1:16

LEVEL 5

What strange vision did Ezekiel once have?

a) a tree in the middle of a tree
b) a box in the middle of a box
c) a wheel in the middle of a wheel
d) a star in the middle of a star

DID YOU KNOW?

Ezekiel had another strange vision, of a valley full of dried-up bones (Ezekiel 37:1–10). God told Ezekiel to speak to the bones, and they came together into skeletons, grew skin, and came back to life. Weird, huh?

BIBLE GOLD

What was Judas Iscariot's pay for betraying Jesus?

a) two new coats
b) five bulls
c) twelve swords
d) thirty silver coins

BIBLE BONUSES

Double Your Chances: B and C

Look in the Book: Matthew 26:14–16

BIBLE GOLD

What was Judas Iscariot's pay for betraying Jesus?

a) two new coats
b) five bulls
c) twelve swords
d) thirty silver coins

DID YOU KNOW?

After Jesus had been arrested and sentenced to death, Judas felt guilty about what he had done and tried to give the money back. Then he went out and killed himself. See for yourself in Matthew 27:3–5.

QUIZ 6

LEVEL 1

What gifts did the wise men bring to the young child Jesus?

a) gold, incense, and myrrh
b) silver, soap, and sandals
c) honey, cheese, and nuts
d) baseballs, footballs, and hockey sticks

BIBLE BONUSES

Double Your Chances: B and D

Look in the Book: Matthew 2:11

LEVEL 1

What gifts did the wise men bring to the young child Jesus?

a) **gold, incense, and myrrh**
b) silver, soap, and sandals
c) honey, cheese, and nuts
d) baseballs, footballs, and hockey sticks

DID YOU KNOW?

Well, you already know what gold is. . .but incense and myrrh are things that smell good!

BIBLE BRONZE

What man's wife turned into a pillar of salt after disobeying God?

a) Lot
b) Moses
c) Peter
d) Bill Clinton

BIBLE BONUSES

Double Your Chances: B and D

Look in the Book: Genesis 19:26

BIBLE BRONZE

What man's wife turned into a pillar of salt after disobeying God?

a) **Lot**
b) Moses
c) Peter
d) Bill Clinton

DID YOU KNOW?

Lot had an uncle named Abraham. . .who started the nation that would be called "Israel."

LEVEL 3

What kind of animal spoke to a prophet named Balaam?

a) a platypus
b) a dog
c) a lion
d) a donkey

BIBLE BONUSES

Double Your Chances: A and B

Look in the Book: Numbers 22:28

LEVEL 3

What kind of animal spoke to a prophet named Balaam?

a) a platypus
b) a dog
c) a lion
d) a donkey

DID YOU KNOW?

One of the judges of Israel, a man named Jair, had thirty sons. . .who rode thirty donkeys! (Judges 10:3–4).

BIBLE SILVER

What did the Holy Spirit look like when it came down on Jesus after His baptism?

a) a dove
b) a cloud
c) a hawk
d) lightning

BIBLE BONUSES

Double Your Chances: B and C

Look in the Book: Luke 3:21–22

BIBLE SILVER

What did the Holy Spirit look like when it came down on Jesus after His baptism?

a) a dove
b) a cloud
c) a hawk
d) lightning

DID YOU KNOW?

Jesus once told His disciples to be "as shrewd [smart] as snakes and as innocent as doves" (Matthew 10:16).

QUIZ 6

LEVEL 5

Who was Solomon's father?

a) Adam
b) Daniel
c) Nehemiah
d) David

BIBLE BONUSES

Double Your Chances: A and C

Look in the Book: 2 Samuel 12:24

LEVEL 5

Who was Solomon's father?

a) Adam
b) Daniel
c) Nehemiah
d) David

DID YOU KNOW?

David and Solomon were both ancestors (early relatives) of Jesus. In Matthew 1:1, Jesus is even called the "son of David," which means that He is an important relative of Israel's great king.

QUIZ 6

BIBLE GOLD

Which of Jesus' twelve disciples was the brother of John?

a) Judas Iscariot
b) Andrew
c) Matthew
d) James

BIBLE BONUSES

Double Your Chances: A and B

Look in the Book: Mark 3:17

BIBLE GOLD

Which of Jesus' twelve disciples was the brother of John?

a) Judas Iscariot
b) Andrew
c) Matthew
d) James

DID YOU KNOW?

Jesus gave James and John a nickname! It wasn't "The J Brothers"—it was *Boanerges*, which means "Sons of Thunder."

QUIZ 1

LEVEL 1

What did Jesus say a wise man builds his house on?

a) a gold mine
b) sand
c) rock
d) a river bank

BIBLE BONUSES

Double Your Chances: A and B

Look in the Book: Luke 6:47–48

LEVEL 1

What did Jesus say a wise man builds his house on?

a) a gold mine
b) sand
c) rock
d) a river bank

DID YOU KNOW?

The apostle Paul called Jesus Christ the "spiritual rock" (1 Corinthians 10:4)—so a wise man builds his life on Jesus.

BIBLE BRONZE

What did God give Daniel the ability to explain?

a) other languages
b) smoke signals
c) dreams
d) the words in rap songs

BIBLE BONUSES

Double Your Chances: A and D

Look in the Book: Daniel 2:23

BIBLE BRONZE

What did God give Daniel the ability to explain?

a) other languages
b) smoke signals
c) dreams
d) the words in rap songs

DID YOU KNOW?

Daniel was also called *Belteshazzar* (Daniel 1:7).

LEVEL 3

What did soldiers put on Jesus' head before His death on the cross?

a) a helmet
b) a golden crown
c) a hood
d) a crown of thorns

BIBLE BONUSES

Double Your Chances: A and C

Look in the Book: Mark 15:16–17

LEVEL 3

What did soldiers put on Jesus' head before His death on the cross?

a) a helmet
b) a golden crown
c) a hood
d) a crown of thorns

DID YOU KNOW?

Some prickly bushes are called "Christ's-thorn" plants.

BIBLE SILVER

What city heard Jonah's preaching and turned to God?

a) Washington, DC
b) Nineveh
c) Jerusalem
d) Rome

BIBLE BONUSES

Double Your Chances: A and C

Look in the Book: Jonah 3:3–5

BIBLE SILVER

What city heard Jonah's preaching and turned to God?

a) Washington, DC
b) Nineveh
c) Jerusalem
d) Rome

DID YOU KNOW?

Nineveh was the capital city of an old country called Assyria. If Nineveh were still a city today, it would be part of Iraq.

QUIZ 1

LEVEL 5

Which of these men did Jesus heal of blindness?

a) Nicodemus
b) Zacchaeus
c) Bartholomew
d) Bartimaeus

BIBLE BONUSES

Double Your Chances: A and B

Look in the Book: Mark 10:46–52

LEVEL 5

Which of these men did Jesus heal of blindness?

a) Nicodemus
b) Zacchaeus
c) Bartholomew
d) Bartimaeus

DID YOU KNOW?

The word "Bar" in a person's name could mean "the son of." So "Bartimaeus" was "the son of Timaeus." What would your "Bar" name be?

BIBLE GOLD

What was special about a man named Enoch?

a) Jesus raised him from the dead.
b) He led Israel as a judge.
c) The apostle Paul healed him of blindness.
d) He never died, because God took him straight to heaven.

BIBLE BONUSES

Double Your Chances: A and B

Look in the Book: Genesis 5:24

BIBLE GOLD

What was special about a man named Enoch?

a) Jesus raised him from the dead.
b) He led Israel as a judge.
c) The apostle Paul healed him of blindness.
d) He never died, because God took him straight to heaven.

DID YOU KNOW?

Theologians (people whose job is to study the Bible) call what happened to Enoch "translation."

QUIZ 8

LEVEL 1

Who gave the five loaves and two fish that Jesus used to feed five thousand people?

a) Long John Silver
b) Peter
c) a little boy
d) Jesus' mother, Mary

BIBLE BONUSES

Double Your Chances: A and D

Look in the Book: John 6:9

LEVEL 1

Who gave the five loaves and two fish that Jesus used to feed five thousand people?

a) Long John Silver
b) Peter
c) a little boy
d) Jesus' mother, Mary

DID YOU KNOW?

Before Jesus handed out food to all the people, He "gave thanks" (John 6:11). That's why it's good for *us* to stop and pray before we eat!

QUIZ 8

BIBLE BRONZE

What kind of contest did Jacob have with God?

a) a chess game
b) a foot race
c) a wrestling match
d) a Bible drill

BIBLE BONUSES

Double Your Chances: A and D

Look in the Book: Genesis 32:24, 30

BIBLE BRONZE

What kind of contest did Jacob have with God?

a) a chess game
b) a foot race
c) a wrestling match
d) a Bible drill

DID YOU KNOW?

Jacob wrestled with God all night. When they were done, God changed Jacob's name to *Israel*—which means "he struggles with God."

QUIZ 8

LEVEL 3

Which of these four problems was *not* a plague on Egypt?

a) chicken pox
b) frogs
c) hail
d) locusts

BIBLE BONUSES

Double Your Chances: C and D

Look in the Book: Exodus 8:2, 9:18, 10:4

LEVEL 3

Which of these four problems was *not* a plague on Egypt?

a) chicken pox
b) frogs
c) hail
d) locusts

DID YOU KNOW?

The word *pox* can mean a terrible evil—or a plague!

BIBLE SILVER

What did Satan tell Jesus to turn into bread?

a) a turtle
b) His sandal
c) a scroll
d) a stone

BIBLE BONUSES

Double Your Chances: A and B

Look in the Book: Luke 4:3

BIBLE SILVER

What did Satan tell Jesus to turn into bread?

a) a turtle
b) His sandal
c) a scroll
d) a stone

DID YOU KNOW?

Satan was trying to make Jesus do something wrong—but Jesus never did anything wrong. Jesus fought back with a Bible verse: "Man does not live on bread alone but on every word that comes from the mouth of the LORD" (Deuteronomy 8:3).

LEVEL 5

What had happened to the man who was helped by the Good Samaritan?

a) He had been struck by lightning.
b) He had fallen over a cliff.
c) He had been bitten by a snake.
d) He had been beaten by robbers.

BIBLE BONUSES

Double Your Chances: A and C

Look in the Book: Luke 10:30

LEVEL 5

What had happened to the man who was helped by the Good Samaritan?

a) He had been struck by lightning.
b) He had fallen over a cliff.
c) He had been bitten by a snake.
d) He had been beaten by robbers.

DID YOU KNOW?

Jesus told the story of the Good Samaritan to explain a verse that says, "Love your neighbor as yourself" (Leviticus 19:18). Jesus was saying that everyone you meet is your neighbor—not just the people who live next door to you.

BIBLE GOLD

Which one of Joseph's brothers kept his other brothers from killing Joseph?

a) Judah
b) Benjamin
c) Dan
d) Reuben

BIBLE BONUSES

Double Your Chances: A and C

Look in the Book: Genesis 37:21

BIBLE GOLD

Which one of Joseph's brothers kept his other brothers from killing Joseph?

a) Judah
b) Benjamin
c) Dan
d) Reuben

DID YOU KNOW?

Reuben was the oldest of Jacob's twelve sons—the men who started the "twelve tribes of Israel." Genesis 49 will tell you more.

QUIZ 9

LEVEL 1

How many commandments—rules to live by—did God give to Moses?

a) 1
b) 10
c) 25
d) 417

BIBLE BONUSES

Double Your Chances: A and D

Look in the Book: Exodus 20:3–17

LEVEL 1

How many commandments—rules to live by—did God give to Moses?

a) 1
b) 10
c) 25
d) 417

DID YOU KNOW?

Only one of the Ten Commandments promises something good to the person who does it: "Honor your father and your mother, so that you may live long in the land the LORD your God is giving you" (Exodus 20:12).

QUIZ 9

BIBLE BRONZE

How long did it take God to create the heavens, the earth, and everything in them?

a) one second
b) twenty-four hours
c) six days
d) one thousand years

BIBLE BONUSES

Double Your Chances: A and D

Look in the Book: Genesis 1:31–2:1

BIBLE BRONZE

How long did it take God to create the heavens, the earth, and everything in them?

a) one second
b) twenty-four hours
c) six days
d) one thousand years

DID YOU KNOW?

God "saved the best for last" and made people on the sixth day of creation. Then He took the seventh day off and rested.

LEVEL 3

What punishment was allowed by Pontius Pilate?

a) Jesus' crucifixion
b) John the Baptist's beheading
c) Paul's stay in jail
d) Daniel's night in the lions' den

BIBLE BONUSES

Double Your Chances: B and C

Look in the Book: Luke 23:23–25

LEVEL 3

What punishment was allowed by Pontius Pilate?

a) **Jesus' crucifixion**
b) John the Baptist's beheading
c) Paul's stay in jail
d) Daniel's night in the lions' den

DID YOU KNOW?

Pontius Pilate's wife told her husband to leave Jesus alone, because she knew He was innocent—but Pilate didn't listen to her (Matthew 27:19–20).

QUIZ 9

BIBLE SILVER

How old was Abraham when his son Isaac was born?

a) 15
b) 30
c) 65
d) 100

BIBLE BONUSES

Double Your Chances: A and B

Look in the Book: Genesis 21:5

BIBLE SILVER

How old was Abraham when his son Isaac was born?

a) 15
b) 30
c) 65
d) 100

DID YOU KNOW?

Abraham's wife, Sarah, was *ninety* years old when Isaac was born (Genesis 17:17). That's pretty old to be having a baby!

LEVEL 5

What miraculous thing did God use to free Paul and Silas from prison?

a) a whirlwind
b) an earthquake
c) a flash flood
d) a swarm of locusts

BIBLE BONUSES

Double Your Chances: C and D

Look in the Book: Acts 16:25–26

LEVEL 5

What miraculous thing did God use to free Paul and Silas from prison?

a) a whirlwind
b) an earthquake
c) a flash flood
d) a swarm of locusts

DID YOU KNOW?

There was an earthquake when Jesus died—Matthew 27:51–52 says, "The earth shook and the rocks split. The tombs broke open and the bodies of many holy people who had died were raised to life." That must have been something to see!

QUIZ 9

BIBLE GOLD

What was the name of Samuel's mother?

a) Mary Magdalene
b) Ruth
c) Hannah
d) Deborah

BIBLE BONUSES

Double Your Chances: A and D

Look in the Book: 1 Samuel 1:20

BIBLE GOLD

What was the name of Samuel's mother?

a) Mary Magdalene
b) Ruth
c) Hannah
d) Deborah

DID YOU KNOW?

The name "Hannah" is a *palindrome*—a word that reads the same way backward or forward. Here are some others: mom, noon, level. Can you think of more?

QUIZ 10

LEVEL 1

How does the Bible describe the tax collector Zacchaeus?

a) short
b) handsome
c) fat
d) smelly

BIBLE BONUSES

Double Your Chances: B and D

Look in the Book: Luke 19:3

LEVEL 1

How does the Bible describe the tax collector Zacchaeus?

a) **short**
b) handsome
c) fat
d) smelly

DID YOU KNOW?

Zacchaeus is one of many "Z" people in the Bible. There were also Zebedee (the father of James and John), Zebulun (a son of Jacob), four Zechariahs (one was the father of John the Baptist), and Zipporah (Moses' wife), to name a few.

BIBLE BRONZE

What kind of bush did God use to get Moses' attention?

a) flowering
b) singing
c) burning
d) walking

BIBLE BONUSES

Double Your Chances: A and B

Look in the Book: Exodus 3:2–3

BIBLE BRONZE

What kind of bush did God use to get Moses' attention?

a) flowering
b) singing
c) burning
d) walking

DID YOU KNOW?

God talked to Moses through the bush—and said that Moses would lead God's people, the Israelites, out of their slavery in Egypt. Read all about it in Exodus 3.

LEVEL 3

What kind of animals was the prodigal son feeding when he decided to go back home?

a) hamsters
b) pigs
c) chickens
d) cows

BIBLE BONUSES

Double Your Chances: A and C

Look in the Book: Luke 15:15–18

LEVEL 3

What kind of animals was the prodigal son feeding when he decided to go back home?

a) hamsters
b) pigs
c) chickens
d) cows

DID YOU KNOW?

"Prodigal" means "wasteful." So the "prodigal son" was a boy who had wasted the money his father had given him.

BIBLE SILVER

What did God do to the people of Babel to keep them from building their giant tower?

a) He made them go blind.
b) He made them fall asleep.
c) He made them speak other languages.
d) He made them afraid of heights.

BIBLE BONUSES

Double Your Chances: B and D

Look in the Book: Genesis 11:8–9

BIBLE SILVER

What did God do to the people of Babel to keep them from building their giant tower?

a) He made them go blind.
b) He made them fall asleep.
c) He made them speak other languages.
d) He made them afraid of heights.

DID YOU KNOW?

Scientists say there may be more than *three thousand* different languages in the world today!

LEVEL 5

What color rope did Rahab put in her window to protect herself and her family?

a) scarlet
b) purple
c) green
d) periwinkle

BIBLE BONUSES

Double Your Chances: B and D

Look in the Book: Joshua 2:21

LEVEL 5

What color rope did Rahab put in her window to protect herself and her family?

a) **scarlet**
b) purple
c) green
d) periwinkle

DID YOU KNOW?

Scarlet is a bright red color.

QUIZ 10

BIBLE GOLD

Who did Peter first meet after an angel broke him out of prison?

a) Lydia
b) Rhoda
c) Salome
d) Julia

BIBLE BONUSES

Double Your Chances: A and D

Look in the Book: Acts 12:13

BIBLE GOLD

Who did Peter first meet after an angel broke him out of prison?

a) Lydia
b) Rhoda
c) Salome
d) Julia

DID YOU KNOW?

The people in Peter's church had been praying hard for Peter, but when Rhoda said Peter was at the door, they didn't believe her. "You're out of your mind," they said (Acts 12:15). They must have forgotten that God answers prayer!

QUIZ 11

LEVEL 1

What did God call Noah's giant boat?

a) an ark
b) a bark
c) a quark
d) *Titanic*

BIBLE BONUSES

Double Your Chances: C and D

Look in the Book: Genesis 6:14

LEVEL 1

What did God call Noah's giant boat?

a) **an ark**
b) a bark
c) a quark
d) *Titanic*

DID YOU KNOW?

A *bark* is a kind of boat, too. . .but a much smaller boat than Noah's!

QUIZ 11

BIBLE BRONZE

How did four men get into a crowded house and bring their paralyzed friend to Jesus?

a) They slid down the chimney.
b) They tunneled through the floor.
c) They cut through the wall.
d) They broke through the roof.

BIBLE BONUSES

Double Your Chances: A and B

Look in the Book: Mark 2:1–5

BIBLE BRONZE

How did four men get into a crowded house and bring their paralyzed friend to Jesus?

a) They slid down the chimney.
b) They tunneled through the floor.
c) They cut through the wall.
d) They broke through the roof.

DID YOU KNOW?

This story happened in Capernaum, the town Jesus lived in after he moved out of Nazareth (Matthew 4:13). Capernaum was on the edge of the Sea of Galilee—where Jesus walked on the water.

QUIZ 11

LEVEL 3

How were Cain and Abel related?

a) father and son
b) brothers
c) cousins
d) just third-grade classmates

BIBLE BONUSES

Double Your Chances: A and D

Look in the Book: Genesis 4:1–2

LEVEL 3

How were Cain and Abel related?

a) father and son
b) brothers
c) cousins
d) just third-grade classmates

DID YOU KNOW?

Cain was Adam and Eve's first son and the first murderer—because he killed his own brother, Abel. Even today, people who cause trouble are said to be "raising Cain."

QUIZ 11

BIBLE SILVER

What instrument did David play to make King Saul feel better?

a) an electric guitar
b) a harp
c) a trumpet
d) a flute

BIBLE BONUSES

Double Your Chances: A and D

Look in the Book: 1 Samuel 16:23

BIBLE SILVER

What instrument did David play to make King Saul feel better?

a) an electric guitar
b) a harp
c) a trumpet
d) a flute

DID YOU KNOW?

God must enjoy harp music, too—the Book of Revelation talks three different times about harps in heaven! Read for yourself in Revelation 5:8, 14:2, and 15:2.

LEVEL 5

What kind of seed did Jesus say the kingdom of heaven was like?

a) dandelion
b) mustard
c) wheat
d) apple

BIBLE BONUSES

Double Your Chances: A and C

Look in the Book: Mark 4:30–32

LEVEL 5

What kind of seed did Jesus say the kingdom of heaven was like?

a) dandelion
b) mustard
c) wheat
d) apple

DID YOU KNOW?

Jesus was saying that His "kingdom," all of the people who would follow Him, was like a tiny seed when it started—it was only Jesus and His twelve disciples. But as they told other people, and those people told even more people, the kingdom of heaven grew like a strong tree. Today, there are millions and millions of Christians around the world!

BIBLE GOLD

What man "prepared the way" for Jesus?

a) Peter
b) Paul
c) John the Baptist
d) Malachi

BIBLE BONUSES

Double Your Chances: A and B

Look in the Book: Matthew 3:1–3

BIBLE GOLD

What man "prepared the way" for Jesus?

a) Peter
b) Paul
c) John the Baptist
d) Malachi

DID YOU KNOW?

Jesus and John the Baptist were relatives—because their mothers, Mary and Elizabeth, were related (Luke 1:36).

QUIZ 12

LEVEL 1

What people first heard the good news about Jesus' birth from an angel?

a) fishermen
b) shepherds
c) soldiers
d) TV reporters

BIBLE BONUSES

Double Your Chances: C and D

Look in the Book: Luke 2:8–11

LEVEL 1

What people first heard the good news about Jesus' birth from an angel?

a) fishermen
b) shepherds
c) soldiers
d) TV reporters

DID YOU KNOW?

In the song "The First Noel," that begins

The first noel the angel did say
was to certain poor shepherds
in fields as they lay,

noel means "Christmas carol."

QUIZ 12

BIBLE BRONZE

What did God tell Abraham to do to his son Isaac?

a) make him eat spinach
b) give him to the priest
c) teach him to play the harp
d) sacrifice him

BIBLE BONUSES

Double Your Chances: A and C

Look in the Book: Genesis 22:2

BIBLE BRONZE

What did God tell Abraham to do to his son Isaac?

a) make him eat spinach
b) give him to the priest
c) teach him to play the harp
d) sacrifice him

DID YOU KNOW?

Abraham is part of the "Faith Hall of Fame" in the book of Hebrews. Hebrews 11:19 says that Abraham was willing to sacrifice Isaac, his only son, because he believed God would raise him back to life. When Abraham proved he was willing to obey, God stopped him and sent a ram to sacrifice instead. Read more in Genesis 22.

QUIZ 12

LEVEL 3

What did Peter see inside a sheet, coming down from heaven by its four corners?

a) animals, reptiles, and birds
b) gold and silver
c) people of many countries
d) Christmas presents

BIBLE BONUSES

Double Your Chances: B and D

Look in the Book: Acts 10:9–12

LEVEL 3

What did Peter see inside a sheet, coming down from heaven by its four corners?

a) **animals, reptiles, and birds**
b) gold and silver
c) people of many countries
d) Christmas presents

DID YOU KNOW?

Peter's vision meant that *all* people should hear the good news about Jesus Christ. God told Peter to kill and eat "unclean" animals, saying "Do not call anything impure that God has made clean" (Acts 10:15). Peter realized that "God. . .accepts men from every nation who fear him and do what is right" (Acts 10:34–35).

QUIZ 12

BIBLE SILVER

What were Egypt's kings called?

a) satraps
b) proconsuls
c) pharaohs
d) scary

BIBLE BONUSES

Double Your Chances: B and D

Look in the Book: Exodus 5:1–4

BIBLE SILVER

What were Egypt's kings called?

a) satraps
b) proconsuls
c) pharaohs
d) scary

DID YOU KNOW?

The name *pharaoh* comes from an Egyptian word that means "the royal palace."

QUIZ 12

LEVEL 5

How long had Lazarus been dead when Jesus brought him back to life?

a) ten minutes
b) twelve hours
c) four days
d) a year

BIBLE BONUSES

Double Your Chances: A and D

Look in the Book: John 11:39–44

LEVEL 5

How long had Lazarus been dead when Jesus brought him back to life?

a) ten minutes
b) twelve hours
c) four days
d) a year

DID YOU KNOW?

There was another man named Lazarus in the Bible. Check out his story in Luke 16:19–31.

QUIZ 12

BIBLE GOLD

Who became the leader of Israel after Moses died?

a) David
b) Joshua
c) Solomon
d) Aaron

BIBLE BONUSES

Double Your Chances: A and C

Look in the Book: Numbers 27:18–20

BIBLE GOLD

Who became the leader of Israel after Moses died?

a) David
b) Joshua
c) Solomon
d) Aaron

DID YOU KNOW?

Joshua's name was actually Hoshea, but Moses changed it (Numbers 13:16). *Joshua* means "Jehovah [God] is salvation."

QUIZ 13

LEVEL 1

What city's walls fell down in front of Joshua's army?

a) Jericho
b) Babylon
c) Tyre
d) Los Angeles

BIBLE BONUSES

Double Your Chances: C and D

Look in the Book: Joshua 6:2–5

LEVEL 1

What city's walls fell down in front of Joshua's army?

a) **Jericho**
b) Babylon
c) Tyre
d) Los Angeles

DID YOU KNOW?

Archaeologists (scientists who study people who lived a long time ago) say Jericho is one of the world's oldest cities.

BIBLE BRONZE

What was Samson famous for?

a) skateboarding skills
b) great strength
c) musical talent
d) writing poems

BIBLE BONUSES

Double Your Chances: A and D

Look in the Book: Judges 16:6

BIBLE BRONZE

What was Samson famous for?

a) skateboarding skills
b) great strength
c) musical talent
d) writing poems

DID YOU KNOW?

Samson was a judge of Israel for twenty years (Judges 15:20). The judges were the leaders of the country in the days before Israel had a king.

LEVEL 3

What did Jesus turn water into, as his very first miracle?

a) Mountain Dew
b) blood
c) oil
d) wine

BIBLE BONUSES

Double Your Chances: A and B

Look in the Book: John 2:1–11

LEVEL 3

What did Jesus turn water into, as his very first miracle?

a) Mountain Dew
b) blood
c) oil
d) wine

DID YOU KNOW?

Jesus performed this miracle at a wedding.

QUIZ 13

BIBLE SILVER

What kind of man was the giant Goliath?

a) a Philadelphian
b) a Philippian
c) a Philistine
d) a philatelist

BIBLE BONUSES

Double Your Chances: A and D

Look in the Book: 1 Samuel 17:23

BIBLE SILVER

What kind of man was the giant Goliath?

a) a Philadelphian
b) a Philippian
c) a Philistine
d) a philatelist

DID YOU KNOW?

Philistines, Philadelphians, and Philippians were all people from the Bible—but *philatelists* are stamp collectors!

LEVEL 5

What place did Matthew leave to follow Jesus?

a) a butcher's shop
b) a tax collector's booth
c) a bakery
d) a boxing ring

BIBLE BONUSES

Double Your Chances: C and D

Look in the Book: Matthew 9:9

LEVEL 5

What place did Matthew leave to follow Jesus?

a) a butcher's shop
b) a tax collector's booth
c) a bakery
d) a boxing ring

DID YOU KNOW?

Matthew was also called *Levi*. One time, Levi invited a bunch of other tax collectors to his house to have dinner with Jesus. Some people complained that Jesus was spending His time with "sinners," but Jesus told them, "It is not the healthy who need a doctor, but the sick. I have not come to call the righteous, but sinners" (Mark 2:17).

BIBLE GOLD

What was the name of Queen Esther's cousin?

a) Mordecai
b) Jeremiah
c) Theophilus
d) Hezekiah

BIBLE BONUSES

Double Your Chances: B and C

Look in the Book: Esther 2:7

BIBLE GOLD

What was the name of Queen Esther's cousin?

a) **Mordecai**
b) Jeremiah
c) Theophilus
d) Hezekiah

DID YOU KNOW?

Mordecai started a holiday, *Purim,* that Jewish people still celebrate each year in February or March. The holiday reminds the Jews of Esther's victory over an evil man named Haman, who wanted to *kill* all the Jews. Read more in Esther 9:23–28.

QUIZ 14

LEVEL 1

Where was Jesus born?

a) Christmas Island
b) Beersheba
c) Jericho
d) Bethlehem

BIBLE BONUSES

Double Your Chances: A and B

Look in the Book: Matthew 2:1

LEVEL 1

Where was Jesus born?

a) Christmas Island
b) Beersheba
c) Jericho
d) Bethlehem

DID YOU KNOW?

A prophet named Micah said that Jesus would be born in Bethlehem—about seven hundred years *before* it happened! Here is Micah 5:2: "But you Bethlehem. . .though you are small among the clans of Judah, out of you will come for me one who will be ruler over Israel, whose origins are from of old, from ancient times."

QUIZ 14

BIBLE BRONZE

What did Jonah do inside the giant fish?

a) practice karate
b) pray
c) cry
d) build a fire

BIBLE BONUSES

Double Your Chances: A and C

Look in the Book: Jonah 2:1

BIBLE BRONZE

What did Jonah do inside the giant fish?

a) practice karate
b) pray
c) cry
d) build a fire

DID YOU KNOW?

In 1 Thessalonians 5:17, the apostle Paul said we should "pray continually," or all the time—not just if we're stuck inside a big fish!

LEVEL 3

What idol did Moses' brother Aaron create for the people of Israel?

a) the Golden Bull
b) the Golden Eagle
c) the Golden Calf
d) the Golden Arches

BIBLE BONUSES

Double Your Chances: B and D

Look in the Book: Exodus 32:3–4

LEVEL 3

What idol did Moses' brother Aaron create for the people of Israel?

a) the Golden Bull
b) the Golden Eagle
c) the Golden Calf
d) the Golden Arches

DID YOU KNOW?

Moses was so mad about this sinful idol that he had the Golden Calf ground into a powder and sprinkled on the water. Then he made the people of Israel drink the water! Check out the whole story in Exodus 32.

BIBLE SILVER

What was the name of the angel who told Mary she would give birth to Jesus?

a) Michael
b) Zadok
c) Gabriel
d) Hananiah

BIBLE BONUSES

Double Your Chances: A and B

Look in the Book: Luke 1:26–31

BIBLE SILVER

What was the name of the angel who told Mary she would give birth to Jesus?

a) Michael
b) Zadok
c) Gabriel
d) Hananiah

DID YOU KNOW?

Gabriel also told a couple named Zechariah and Elizabeth that they would have a special son named John the Baptist. Find out more in Luke 1:5–25.

QUIZ 14

LEVEL 5

What kind of animals helped Samson burn the grain fields of his enemies?

a) lightning bugs
b) lions
c) donkeys
d) foxes

BIBLE BONUSES

Double Your Chances: A and C

Look in the Book: Judges 15:3–5

LEVEL 5

What kind of animals helped Samson burn the grain fields of his enemies?

a) lightning bugs
b) lions
c) donkeys
d) foxes

DID YOU KNOW?

Foxes live in holes—that's what Jesus said in Matthew 8:20: "Foxes have holes and birds of the air have nests, but the Son of Man has no place to lay his head."

BIBLE GOLD

What does Golgotha, where Jesus was killed on a cross, mean?

a) The Place of the Dead
b) The Place of Sadness
c) The Place of Fear
d) The Place of the Skull

BIBLE BONUSES

Double Your Chances: A and C

Look in the Book: Matthew 27:33

BIBLE GOLD

What does Golgotha, where Jesus was killed on a cross, mean?

a) The Place of the Dead
b) The Place of Sadness
c) The Place of Fear
d) The Place of the Skull

DID YOU KNOW?

When Jesus was on the cross, the sun went dark for three hours—from noon until 3 P.M. (Luke 23:44–45). Do you think that might have caught some people's attention? Even one of the Roman soldiers who was guarding Jesus said, "Surely this was a righteous man" (Luke 23:47).

QUIZ 15

LEVEL 1

How did Moses and the people of Israel cross the Red Sea?

a) in an airplane
b) in boats
c) they swam
d) they walked across on dry land

BIBLE BONUSES

Double Your Chances: A and B

Look in the Book: Exodus 14:21–22

LEVEL 1

How did Moses and the people of Israel cross the Red Sea?

a) in an airplane
b) in boats
c) they swam
d) they walked across on dry land

DID YOU KNOW?

This wasn't the only time the people of Israel walked across a body of water on dry ground. Joshua once led the people across the Jordan River the same way (Joshua 3:13–17).

BIBLE BRONZE

Where did Jesus say we should store our treasure?

a) in heaven
b) in a bank
c) in a cave
d) in a pirate's chest

BIBLE BONUSES

Double Your Chances: B and D

Look in the Book: Matthew 6:20

BIBLE BRONZE

Where did Jesus say we should store our treasure?

a) **in heaven**
b) in a bank
c) in a cave
d) in a pirate's chest

DID YOU KNOW?

The apostle Paul told people how to store up treasure in heaven: "Command them to do good, to be rich in good deeds, and to be generous and willing to share. In this way they will lay up treasure for themselves as a firm foundation for the coming age" (1 Timothy 6:18–19).

LEVEL 3

Who had a dream about angels going up and down a ladder to heaven?

a) Noah
b) Jacob
c) Daniel
d) Habakkuk

BIBLE BONUSES

Double Your Chances: C and D

Look in the Book: Genesis 28:10–12

LEVEL 3

Who had a dream about angels going up and down a ladder to heaven?

a) Noah
b) Jacob
c) Daniel
d) Habakkuk

DID YOU KNOW?

African-American slaves used this story to make up a song—called a "spiritual"—that went like this:

We are climbing Jacob's ladder,
we are climbing Jacob's ladder,
we are climbing Jacob's ladder,
soldiers of the cross.

BIBLE SILVER

Why did Jesus use a whip to drive people out of the temple?

a) They were making too much noise.
b) They were using God's house as a marketplace.
c) They were drinking wine.
d) They were drawing pictures on their bulletins.

BIBLE BONUSES

Double Your Chances: A and D

Look in the Book: John 2:13–16

BIBLE SILVER

Why did Jesus use a whip to drive people out of the temple?

a) They were making too much noise.
b) They were using God's house as a marketplace.
c) They were drinking wine.
d) They were drawing pictures on their bulletins.

DID YOU KNOW?

When the disciples saw Jesus chase the sellers out of the temple, they remembered a verse from the Psalms: "Zeal for your house consumes me" (Psalm 69:9). That meant Jesus' concern about the temple "ate Him up."

LEVEL 5

What was Esau really good at doing?

a) hunting
b) swimming
c) woodworking
d) rodeo riding

BIBLE BONUSES

Double Your Chances: C and D

Look in the Book: Genesis 25:27

LEVEL 5

What was Esau really good at doing?

a) **hunting**
b) swimming
c) woodworking
d) rodeo riding

DID YOU KNOW?

The Bible talks about two other men who were good at hunting: Ishmael, a son of Abraham, who "lived in the desert and became an archer" (Genesis 21:20), and Nimrod, "a mighty hunter before the LORD" (Genesis 10:9).

BIBLE GOLD

What couple died after lying to Peter about an offering they made?

a) Hosea and Gomer
b) Aquila and Priscilla
c) Ananias and Sapphira
d) Ruth and Boaz

BIBLE BONUSES

Look in the Book: Acts 5:1–10

Double Your Chances: B and D

BIBLE GOLD

What couple died after lying to Peter about an offering they made?

a) Hosea and Gomer
b) Aquila and Priscilla
c) Ananias and Sapphira
d) Ruth and Boaz

DID YOU KNOW?

The deaths of Ananias and Sapphira put a real scare into the people who knew them. In Acts 5:11, Luke says, "Great fear seized the whole church and all who heard about these events."

QUIZ 16

LEVEL 1

What kind of animal tempted Eve to eat the fruit that God said she should not eat?

a) serpent
b) hawk
c) horse
d) hippopotamus

BIBLE BONUSES

Double Your Chances: B and D

Look in the Book: Genesis 3:1–5

LEVEL 1

What kind of animal tempted Eve to eat the fruit that God said she should not eat?

a) **serpent**
b) hawk
c) horse
d) hippopotamus

DID YOU KNOW?

Many people think that the fruit Adam and Eve ate was an apple—but the Bible doesn't say that. The fruit came from "the tree of the knowledge of good and evil" (Genesis 2:17), and nobody knows what that tree's fruit looks like!

BIBLE BRONZE

What fancy piece of clothing did Joseph receive from his father, Jacob?

a) a robe
b) a hat
c) a belt
d) a necktie

BIBLE BONUSES

Double Your Chances: B and D

Look in the Book: Genesis 37:3

BIBLE BRONZE

What fancy piece of clothing did Joseph receive from his father, Jacob?

a) **a robe**
b) a hat
c) a belt
d) a necktie

DID YOU KNOW?

Joseph was the second youngest of Jacob's twelve sons—and he was Daddy's favorite. Joseph's ten older brothers hated him because of that and actually thought about killing Joseph. In the end, they sold him as a slave—but that turned out to be a good thing. The whole story is in the last fourteen chapters of Genesis.

LEVEL 3

How did God take Elijah up to heaven?

a) in a hot air balloon
b) on the arm of an angel
c) in a whirlwind
d) on the back of an eagle

BIBLE BONUSES

Double Your Chances: A and D

Look in the Book: 2 Kings 2:11

LEVEL 3

How did God take Elijah up to heaven?

a) in a hot air balloon
b) on the arm of an angel
c) **in a whirlwind**
d) on the back of an eagle

DID YOU KNOW?

A prophet called Nahum once wrote about God's power, saying that "His way is in the whirlwind and the storm, and clouds are the dust of his feet" (Nahum 1:3). But Nahum also said that "The LORD is good, a refuge in times of trouble. He cares for those who trust in him" (Nahum 1:7).

QUIZ 16

BIBLE SILVER

How many of the ten lepers that Jesus healed remembered to thank God?

a) all ten
b) nine
c) only one
d) none

BIBLE BONUSES

Double Your Chances: A and D

Look in the Book: Luke 17:12–19

BIBLE SILVER

How many of the ten lepers that Jesus healed remembered to thank God?

a) all ten
b) nine
c) only one
d) none

DID YOU KNOW?

The apostle Paul said we should be thankful all the time—for good things and even for the not-so-good things—because "this is God's will for you in Christ Jesus" (1 Thessalonians 5:18).

LEVEL 5

What color cloth was sold by Lydia, who became a Christian after hearing Paul's preaching?

a) red
b) blue
c) brown
d) purple

BIBLE BONUSES

Double Your Chances: B and C

Look in the Book: Acts 16:14

LEVEL 5

What color cloth was sold by Lydia, who became a Christian after hearing Paul's preaching?

a) red
b) blue
c) brown
d) purple

DID YOU KNOW?

In Bible times, people who wore purple clothes were often the rich and powerful. Remember Mordecai in the story of Esther? When he pleased the king, he was given "royal garments [clothes] of blue and white, a large crown of gold and a purple robe of fine linen" (Esther 8:15).

BIBLE GOLD

What was Saul looking for when he learned he would become the king of Israel?

a) a wife
b) lost donkeys
c) water
d) a job

BIBLE BONUSES

Double Your Chances: A and D

Look in the Book: 1 Samuel 10:1–2

BIBLE GOLD

What was Saul looking for when he learned he would become the king of Israel?

a) a wife
b) lost donkeys
c) water
d) a job

DID YOU KNOW?

One time, Jesus told a story about lost *sheep*—saying that a shepherd with one hundred sheep would leave ninety-nine of them to go find the one that had wandered away. He was saying that God goes out of His way to look for us, and make us part of His family. Read more in Matthew 18:10–14.

QUIZ 17

LEVEL 1

From what dangerous place did God rescue Shadrach, Meschach, and Abednego?

a) a rushing river
b) a fiery furnace
c) a collapsing cave
d) a teetering treehouse

BIBLE BONUSES

Double Your Chances: C and D

Look in the Book: Daniel 3:26–28

LEVEL 1

From what dangerous place did God rescue Shadrach, Meschach, and Abednego?

a) a rushing river
b) a fiery furnace
c) a collapsing cave
d) a teetering treehouse

DID YOU KNOW?

Shadrach, Meschach, and Abednego were all friends of Daniel—the guy who spent a night in the lions' den. They all lived together while they served the king of Babylon (Daniel 2:49).

BIBLE BRONZE

Who named all of the animals?

a) God
b) Adam
c) Noah
d) Zack the Zookeeper

BIBLE BONUSES

Double Your Chances: A and D

Look in the Book: Genesis 2:19

BIBLE BRONZE

Who named all of the animals?

a) God
b) Adam
c) Noah
d) Zack the Zookeeper

DID YOU KNOW?

Adam named all the animals just before God gave him Eve as his wife. As nice as the animals were, none of them was a "suitable helper" for Adam (Genesis 2:20). So, before long, God made Adam fall into a deep sleep, took a rib from his side, and formed Eve to be Adam's wife.

QUIZ 11

LEVEL 3

What did Jesus say little children should do?

a) "Be quiet in church!"
b) "Come to me."
c) "Read your Bibles."
d) "Obey your parents."

BIBLE BONUSES

Double Your Chances: A and C

Look in the Book: Matthew 19:14

LEVEL 3

What did Jesus say little children should do?

a) "Be quiet in church!"
b) "Come to me."
c) "Read your Bibles."
d) "Obey your parents."

DID YOU KNOW?

The song "Jesus Loves Me," which talks a lot about little children and Jesus, is more than one hundred years old! The first verse of the song was written in 1860, just before the American Civil War.

QUIZ 11

BIBLE SILVER

What kind of birds fed the prophet Elijah when he was hiding from King Ahab?

a) eagles
b) storks
c) hummingbirds
d) ravens

BIBLE BONUSES

Double Your Chances: B and C

Look in the Book: 1 Kings 17:1–6

BIBLE SILVER

What kind of birds fed the prophet Elijah when he was hiding from King Ahab?

a) eagles
b) storks
c) hummingbirds
d) ravens

DID YOU KNOW?

Jesus once talked about ravens, saying, "They do not sow or reap, they have no storeroom or barn; yet God feeds them" (Luke 12:24). Then Jesus said, "And how much more valuable you are than birds!"

LEVEL 5

What did the sign on the cross say that Jesus was king of?

a) the heavens
b) the world
c) the Jews
d) the universe

BIBLE BONUSES

Double Your Chances: A and B

Look in the Book: John 19:19

LEVEL 5

What did the sign on the cross say that Jesus was king of?

a) the heavens
b) the world
c) the Jews
d) the universe

DID YOU KNOW?

In Revelation 19:16, Jesus is called "KING OF KINGS AND LORD OF LORDS"—it's even written on His clothes!

BIBLE GOLD

What king had Daniel thrown into the lions' den?

a) Darius
b) Nebuchadnezzar
c) Ahab
d) Herod

BIBLE BONUSES

Double Your Chances: B and D

Look in the Book: Daniel 6:16–25

BIBLE GOLD

What king had Daniel thrown into the lions' den?

a) **Darius**
b) Nebuchadnezzar
c) Ahab
d) Herod

DID YOU KNOW?

King Darius, who really liked Daniel, had been tricked into passing a law that said everyone should pray to *him*—but when Daniel kept praying to God, the king couldn't change the law. The good news is that Daniel came out just fine—"My God sent his angel, and he shut the mouths of the lions," Daniel said. "They have not hurt me" (Daniel 6:22).

QUIZ 18

LEVEL 1

Where did Adam and Eve live until God made them move out?

a) the Mountain of Eden
b) the Valley of Eden
c) the Garden of Eden
d) the Hotel of Eden

BIBLE BONUSES

Double Your Chances: A and D

Look in the Book: Genesis 2:8

LEVEL 1

Where did Adam and Eve live until God made them move out?

a) the Mountain of Eden
b) the Valley of Eden
c) the Garden of Eden
d) the Hotel of Eden

DID YOU KNOW?

After Adam and Eve had to leave the Garden of Eden, angels and a flaming sword kept them out (Genesis 3:24).

BIBLE BRONZE

What job did King David have when he was just a boy?

a) shepherd
b) baker
c) carpenter
d) paperboy

BIBLE BONUSES

Double Your Chances: B and D

Look in the Book: 1 Samuel 16:11–13

BIBLE BRONZE

What job did King David have when he was just a boy?

a) **shepherd**
b) baker
c) carpenter
d) paperboy

DID YOU KNOW?

Later in his life, David wrote the famous words of Psalm 23: "The LORD is my shepherd. . . ."

LEVEL 3

Where did baby Moses' mother hide a basket holding her little boy?

a) in the Nile River
b) in a treetop
c) in a cave
d) in the trunk of her car

BIBLE BONUSES

Look in the Book: Exodus 2:3

Double Your Chances: B and D

LEVEL 3

Where did baby Moses' mother hide a basket holding her little boy?

a) **in the Nile River**
b) in a treetop
c) in a cave
d) in the trunk of her car

DID YOU KNOW?

The Nile is the longest river in the world—more than 4,100 miles long!

QUIZ 18

BIBLE SILVER

How did Jesus calm a storm on the sea?

a) He spoke to the storm.
b) He touched the water with a stick.
c) He waved His arms over the sea.
d) He dipped His robe into the water.

BIBLE BONUSES

Double Your Chances: B and C

Look in the Book: Mark 4:39

BIBLE SILVER

How did Jesus calm a storm on the sea?

a) **He spoke to the storm.**
b) He touched the water with a stick.
c) He waved His arms over the sea.
d) He dipped His robe into the water.

DID YOU KNOW?

Psalm 107 says that God both starts and stops the storm! "For he spoke and stirred up a tempest [storm] that lifted high the waves" (verse 25); later, God "stilled the storm to a whisper; the waves of the sea were hushed" (verse 29).

QUIZ 18

LEVEL 5

What kind of animal did God give Abraham to sacrifice, instead of his son, Isaac?

a) a bull
b) a sparrow
c) a lamb
d) a ram

BIBLE BONUSES

Double Your Chances: B and C

Look in the Book: Genesis 22:13–14

LEVEL 5

What kind of animal did God give Abraham to sacrifice, instead of his son, Isaac?

a) a bull
b) a sparrow
c) a lamb
d) a ram

DID YOU KNOW?

Rams are like sheep, but they have big curved horns on their heads.

QUIZ 18

BIBLE GOLD

Who was Rachel's older sister, who also married Jacob?

a) Leah
b) Deborah
c) Salome
d) Phoebe

BIBLE BONUSES

Double Your Chances: C and D

Look in the Book: Genesis 29:25–27

BIBLE GOLD

Who was Rachel's older sister, who also married Jacob?

a) **Leah**
b) Deborah
c) Salome
d) Phoebe

DID YOU KNOW?

Rachel and Leah's father tricked Jacob into marrying *both* girls—even though Jacob really loved Rachel (Genesis 29:14–30). When Jacob showed more love to Rachel than to Leah, it caused a lot of problems in the family. Later, Jacob would cause more problems by choosing a favorite son—by loving Joseph more than his eleven other boys.

QUIZ 19

LEVEL 1

What weapon did David use to knock down the giant Goliath?

a) a machine gun
b) a bow and arrow
c) a spear
d) a slingshot

BIBLE BONUSES

Double Your Chances: A and C

Look in the Book: 1 Samuel 17:49–50

LEVEL 1

What weapon did David use to knock down the giant Goliath?

a) a machine gun
b) a bow and arrow
c) a spear
d) a slingshot

DID YOU KNOW?

David had five stones to use in his slingshot (1 Samuel 17:40)—but he only needed one (verses 48–50)!

BIBLE BRONZE

Which disciple walked on water with Jesus?

a) Philip
b) Matthew
c) Thomas
d) Peter

BIBLE BONUSES

Double Your Chances: A and C

Look in the Book: Matthew 14:29

BIBLE BRONZE

Which disciple walked on water with Jesus?

a) Philip
b) Matthew
c) Thomas
d) Peter

DID YOU KNOW?

Peter could be very brave—from the time he walked on the water to the time he fought to protect Jesus. On the night Jesus was arrested, Peter grabbed a sword and hit a man named Malchus, cutting off his ear (John 18:10). Lucky for Malchus, Jesus healed him right away (Luke 22:50–51).

LEVEL 3

How did Delilah make Samson weak?

a) She got him drunk.
b) She had his head shaved.
c) She poisoned his food.
d) She gave him a big kiss.

BIBLE BONUSES

Double Your Chances: A and D

Look in the Book: Judges 16:18–19

LEVEL 3

How did Delilah make Samson weak?

a) She got him drunk.
b) She had his head shaved.
c) She poisoned his food.
d) She gave him a big kiss.

DID YOU KNOW?

Samson was called a "Nazirite"—a person who served God in special ways. The Nazirite rules said that Samson should never cut his hair (Judges 13:5). When his head was shaved, Samson lost the strength God had given him.

BIBLE SILVER

What did Esau sell to his brother Jacob for a bowl of stew?

a) his birthplace
b) his birthright
c) his birthstone
d) his birth certificate

BIBLE BONUSES

Double Your Chances: A and C

Look in the Book: Genesis 25:29–34

BIBLE SILVER

What did Esau sell to his brother Jacob for a bowl of stew?

a) his birthplace
b) his birthright
c) his birthstone
d) his birth certificate

DID YOU KNOW?

The birthright was a blessing especially for the oldest son in a family. One king of Judah, a man named Jehoshaphat, gave his sons "many gifts of silver and gold and articles of value, as well as fortified cities in Judah, but he had given the kingdom to Jehoram because he was his first-born son" (2 Chronicles 21:3).

QUIZ 19

LEVEL 5

How many days did Jesus fast—go without eating—while the devil was tempting Him?

a) 1
b) 12
c) 40
d) 365

BIBLE BONUSES

Double Your Chances: A and D

Look in the Book: Luke 4:1–2

LEVEL 5

How many days did Jesus fast—go without eating—while the devil was tempting Him?

a) 1
b) 12
c) 40
d) 365

DID YOU KNOW?

Moses fasted forty days, too—when God was giving him the Ten Commandments on Mount Sinai (Exodus 34:28).

QUIZ 19

BIBLE GOLD

What did the mother of James and John once ask Jesus?

a) that her sons would never die
b) that her sons could sit at Jesus' side in heaven
c) that her sons could turn stones into gold
d) that her sons would have many children

BIBLE BONUSES

Double Your Chances: A and C

Look in the Book: Matthew 20:21

BIBLE GOLD

What did the mother of James and John once ask Jesus?

a) that her sons would never die
b) that her sons could sit at Jesus' side in heaven
c) that her sons could turn stones into gold
d) that her sons would have many children

DID YOU KNOW?

The other disciples got mad when they heard what James and John's mother asked—so Jesus taught them about how to be *really* important. "Whoever wants to become great among you," Jesus said, "must be your servant" (Matthew 20:26).

QUIZ 20

LEVEL 1

What kind of bird called out after Peter denied Jesus the third time?

a) a rooster
b) an eagle
c) a blue jay
d) a killdeer

BIBLE BONUSES

Double Your Chances: A and B

Look in the Book: Matthew 26:73–75

LEVEL 1

What kind of bird called out after Peter denied Jesus the third time?

a) a rooster
b) an eagle
c) a blue jay
d) a killdeer

DID YOU KNOW?

Jesus knew ahead of time that Peter would say he didn't even know Jesus (look at Matthew 26:33–34). After Peter denied Jesus, he remembered what Jesus had said—and Peter felt so bad that he began to cry (Matthew 26:75).

QUIZ 20

BIBLE BRONZE

What did God put in the sky as a promise never again to destroy the earth with a flood?

a) birds
b) the moon
c) a rainbow
d) the space shuttle

BIBLE BONUSES

Double Your Chances: A and D

Look in the Book: Genesis 9:13–16

BIBLE BRONZE

What did God put in the sky as a promise never again to destroy the earth with a flood?

a) birds
b) the moon
c) a rainbow
d) the space shuttle

DID YOU KNOW?

There's a rainbow above God's throne in heaven! See for yourself in Ezekiel 1:28 and Revelation 4:3.

LEVEL 3

What kind of bug does Proverbs say is an example for lazy people?

a) jitterbug
b) moth
c) grasshopper
d) ant

BIBLE BONUSES

Double Your Chances: A and C

Look in the Book: Proverbs 6:6–8

LEVEL 3

What kind of bug does Proverbs say is an example for lazy people?

a) jitterbug
b) moth
c) grasshopper
d) ant

DID YOU KNOW?

Some ants are just like farmers! One kind of ant chews up green leaves to make a "garden" that grows fungus to eat. Another kind of ant keeps "cows"—actually, bugs called *aphids*—and drinks the juice the aphid makes.

BIBLE SILVER

Why did King Xerxes choose a girl named Esther to be his queen?

a) She was smart.
b) She was beautiful.
c) She was rich.
d) She was a good cook.

BIBLE BONUSES

Double Your Chances: C and D

Look in the Book: Esther 2:17

BIBLE SILVER

Why did King Xerxes choose a girl named Esther to be his queen?

a) She was smart.
b) She was beautiful.
c) She was rich.
d) She was a good cook.

DID YOU KNOW?

Esther also had another name—*Hadassah* (Esther 2:7).

LEVEL 5

How did Jesus go up to heaven forty days after He came back to life from the dead?

a) on the arm of an angel
b) in a cloud
c) in a golden chariot
d) on the wings of an eagle

BIBLE BONUSES

Double Your Chances: A and D

Look in the Book: Acts 1:9

LEVEL 5

How did Jesus go up to heaven forty days after He came back to life from the dead?

a) on the arm of an angel
b) in a cloud
c) in a golden chariot
d) on the wings of an eagle

DID YOU KNOW?

Jesus will come back to earth again in the same way! Angels told the people who watched Jesus go up to heaven that He would "come back in the same way" (Acts 1:11). And Jesus Himself once said, "In the future, you will see the Son of Man [Jesus]. . .coming on the clouds of heaven" (Matthew 26:64).

BIBLE GOLD

What sin had Moses committed when he was a young man in Egypt?

a) He had called Pharaoh a bad name.
b) He had killed an Egyptian.
c) He had stolen Pharaoh's money.
d) He had lied to his mother.

BIBLE BONUSES

Double Your Chances: A and D

Look in the Book: Exodus 2:11–12

BIBLE GOLD

What sin had Moses committed when he was a young man in Egypt?

a) He had called Pharaoh a bad name.
b) He had killed an Egyptian.
c) He had stolen Pharaoh's money.
d) He had lied to his mother.

DID YOU KNOW?

Moses was the adopted grandson of the Egyptian pharaoh—because the pharaoh's daughter made Moses her son after she found him in a basket in the Nile River (Exodus 2:9).

LIKE BIBLE TRIVIA?

Then check out these great books from Barbour Publishing!

The Bible Detective by Carol Smith

Solve mysteries posed by a mixed-up story using biblical characters, places, and quotations.

ISBN 1-57748-838-5

Paperback/224 pages $2.97

My Final Answer by Paul Kent

Thirty separate quizzes feature twelve multiple choice questions each—and the questions get progressively harder!

ISBN 1-58660-030-3

Paperback/256 pages $2.97

Bible IQ by Rayburn Ray

One hundred sections of ten questions each—and a systematic scoring system to tell you just how well you did.

ISBN 1-57748-837-7

Paperback/256 pages $2.97

Test Your Bible Knowledge by Carl Shoup

Over 1,400 multiple-choice questions to test your mettle, tickle your funny bone, and tantalize your intellect.

ISBN 1-55748-541-0

Paperback/224 pages $2.97

Fun Facts about the Bible by Robyn Martins

Challenging and intriguing Bible trivia—expect some of the answers to surprise you! ISBN 1-55748-897-5

Paperback/256 pages $2.97

Available wherever books are sold.
Or order from:

Barbour Publishing, Inc.
P.O. Box 719
Uhrichsville, OH 44683
http://www.barbourbooks.com

If you order by mail add $2.00 to your order for shipping.
Prices subject to change without notice.